THE STORY ALTON TOWERS

Jack O'Callaghan

To Mum and Dad

For joining me on my journey to explore
my theme park obsession.

To Ben

For sharing my passion for rollercoasters and theme parks.
Everything is better with friends to share it with.

To Josh and Megan

For helping me to take this book from an idea into
an enjoyable and fascinating read for everybody.
I can't say thank you enough for your help.

COPYRIGHT INFORMATION

PREFACE TO THE FIRST EDITION

Dear reader,

Thank you so much for purchasing this book! I appreciate it more than you can imagine. I hope that you enjoy reading *The Story of Alton Towers*. If you do, then please consider leaving a review for the book on Amazon. If you find any mistakes within the book, then please contact me at **feedback.altontowersstory@gmail.com** so that these can be rectified.

I intend to use any feedback to shape any further editions of this book, so please do not hesitate to contact me if you find anything that can be improved upon. I believe that nothing is ever perfect, and there are always things that you can do to improve your work.

Thanks,
Jack

CONTENTS

INTRODUCTION

Although the Towers only opened as a theme park in 1980, Alton Towers has been open to the public since the early 19th century. The iconic Towers ruins make Alton Towers one of the most unique theme parks in the world. The park is a place of decorum and great historical importance, yet also a champion of the most immersive rollercoaster experiences in the world…

How did the Towers estate pass from the ownership of the well-respected Earls of Shrewsbury to the hands of businessman John Broome? And how did Alton Towers work with the toughest planning restrictions in the world, and yet still create the most innovative rides found in any park on the globe?

Within this book, you can discover how Alton Towers developed from a small hunting lodge to one of the most popular and iconic theme parks in the world. You can learn how Alton Towers developed as it changed ownership, and how the influence of these owners helped to shape the park we see today.

THE STORY OF ALTON TOWERS

PART I: FROM ALVETON LODGE TO ALTON TOWERS

CHAPTER ONE: ALVETON LODGE

We can trace the origins of Alton Towers back to 716 A.D. when the grounds were involved in a great battle between the Saxon Kings Ceolred of Mercia and Ine of Wessex. In around 700 A.D. King Ceolred of Mercia built an Iron-Age Fortress on Bunbury Hill, which lay on where the present grounds of Alton Towers are situated. King Ceolred of Mercia is commonly confused for his relative and predecessor, Coenred of Mercia.

The site of this fortress was besieged in 716 A.D. by King Ine of Wessex, and a battle followed. The result of this great battle was a stalemate, at the cost of a great number of lives.

This led to the site supposedly being dubbed Slain Hollow by locals, because of the many soldiers who died at the site of that great battle in 716 A.D. However, some authors also suggest that Victorian Romanticism had an influence on the name Slain Hollow, of the original name Slade Dale – describing a wooded hollow.

The Towers passed between many hands until, in 1406, Sir John Talbot (the First Earl of Shrewsbury) gained ownership of the estate through marriage. The Talbots were the most influential family in the History of Alton Towers; the family held the estate for well over 500 years and are accountable for the Gothic style of the Towers seen today...

* * *

At the start of the 17th century, the Shrewsbury family began works to build a modest hunting lodge on their estate, by the name of Alveton Lodge. Although the Shrewsbury family lived primarily in Oxfordshire, Alveton Lodge was set in the beautiful Peak District, deep into the sprawling Staffordshire countryside. It is no wonder that Alveton Lodge was the summer residence of the Shrewsbury family- such was its charming beauty. Set deep into rural Staffordshire, Alveton Lodge was a charming summer home at that, and one that the Earls of Shrewsbury would strive to enhance for generations to come.

There is much ambiguity regarding the completion of Alveton Lodge, although a book by Dr Robert Plot in 1686 refers to the Lodge as the 'Old Lodge'. This suggests that the lodge was likely completed many years before the publication of Dr Plot's book. Until the late 19th Century, the family only used the lodge for occasional summer visits. However, the Fifteenth Earl of Shrewsbury, Charles Talbot (1753-1827), took an increasing interest in the Alton estate and continual improvements were being executed to the lodge.

The estate was jointly owned between the Shrewsbury and Burton families. In October 1807, the Fifteenth Earl of Shrewsbury, Charles Talbot, bought out the Burtons' ownership of the estate. From this point onwards, he was free to develop the property as he deemed fit. The purchase of the entire Alveton estate is a hugely important landmark in the history of the Lodge, as it marks the point at which the Fifteenth Earl started placing an increasing amount of importance on the estate.

This interest in Alveton Lodge continued to grow and from 1814, the Earl made Alveton Lodge (Alveton being old English for Alton) his primary residence for himself and his wife.

CHAPTER TWO: ALTON ABBEY

A s early as the start of the 19 Century, the Fifteenth Earl of Shrewsbury had placed more emphasis towards Alveton Lodge. Since 1807, the Earl had been the sole owner of the estate, having bought out the Burtons' share of the lodge, had expanded the grounds as he deemed fit. In 1811, financial accounts for the lodge had become known as the Abbey Accounts, rather than the Lodge Accounts.

Alton Abbey was not related to any religious group, although the Earls of Shrewsbury came from an extensive line of devout Catholics. Alton Abbey was of a far grander scale than that of Alveton Lodge, reflected by the increasing costs of building work on the Abbey. From £550 in the year of 1811, the costs of building work had risen to over £3,500 by 1813.

❊ ❊ ❊

The North front of Alton Abbey was constructed, which is still remarkably like the view of Alton Towers that visitors experience when entering the park to this day. From 1813, work was completed on the grand entrance to the Towers, which remains very much visible to people from the North view of the Towers.

Around the 1820s, work had been finished on the grand entrance hall to the Towers. Featuring a charming spiral staircase, beautiful ornate balustrades, honourable paintings of ancestral members, and a roaring fireplace of commanding grandeur. This entrance hall displayed the magnificent nature of Alton Abbey to visitors.

❊ ❊ ❊

In 1824, the Conservatories were completed at Alton Abbey. The Conservatories were built to extend the Abbey and were connected to the existing principal drawing-room. Located in the gardens, the Conservatories gave a magnificent view of the scenic landscape below. The glass Conservatories added a touch of charm to the gardens and were used in those days to grow bananas within the gardens.

Bananas were considered to be an exotic fruit in those days and were popular amongst wealthy members of society. In 1834 the Sixteenth Earl even sent a banana, with instructions of how to eat it, to the Duke of Devonshire.

CHAPTER THREE: ALTON TOWERS

Although it is difficult to suggest a single point at which Alton Abbey became Alton Towers, it would be the Sixteenth Earl of Shrewsbury, the great Fifteenth Earl's nephew, who would be the first to refer to the estate by the name of the Towers. It was after his uncle's death in 1827 that the Sixteenth Earl would take ownership of the estate. Therefore, the change can be suggested to have occurred around the early 1830s.

* * *

The Fifteenth Earl was responsible for much of the transformation that had occurred at Alton. Water had been moved from a nearby spring to create the park's majestic lake. The lake lies in front of the Towers as visitors enter the park today when passing down Towers Street. The gothic style, which gives Alton Towers its unrivalled beauty, was the great decorative work of Charles Talbot.

In honour of the Fifteenth Earl and his dedication to improving the landscape of the Alton estate, a replica was made of the Choragic Monument of Athens. On it was the inscription "He Made the Desert Smile", a reference to the transformation of the previously barren landscape into a lush haven of all flora and fauna, by the work of the Fifteenth Earl…

According to a 40th-anniversary guide of Alton Towers' gardens, the large green S made of a styled hedge, which lies directly below the monument, was taken from a design found on a fireplace within the Towers themselves-likely a proud family reference to the title which the great Earls inherited: the Earls of Shrewsbury.

* * *

A.W.N. Pugin was born at Bedford Square at the heart of London on 1st March 1812 and would grow up to be one of the most celebrated architects in British history. During his youth, young Pugin would frequently travel with his father, taking sketches of many buildings in both England, where he gained much knowledge of medieval architecture, and in Paris, where he would expand his knowledge when visiting the stunning Churches in France.

Pugin's mother and father both died in 1832, the same year in which he would first meet the Sixteenth Earl of Shrewsbury, John Talbot. The late Earl had great aspirations for the future of Alton Towers, and ultimately A.W.N Pugin would have a tremendous impact on that future. (It would not be, however, until late 1837 that Pugin would first visit Alton Towers)

* * *

Pugin was to become the most celebrated gothic revival architect in British history and would champion the creation of the splendid view with which guests to the park are presented with when visiting the Towers today.

Pugin would oversee the construction of a new entrance hall, dining hall, chapel, the Talbot gallery, and most other extensions that would occur at Alton Towers. Pugin's gothic style fascinated the Sixteenth Earl and would make Alton Towers such a fascination to the public in later years.

Pugin's magnificent work at Alton Towers would then continue until his death on 14 September 1852. Dying because of a nervous breakdown after overworking himself, Pugin died at 40 years of age. However, his work during his lifetime would leave a legacy in architecture for years to come.

"Nothing can be more dangerous than looking at prints of buildings, and trying to imitate bits of them. These architectural books are as bad as the Scriptures in the hands of the Protestants."

- AUGUSTUS WELBY NORTHMORE PUGIN

❊ ❊ ❊

English architect Robert Abraham completed the Chinese Pagoda Fountain circa 1830. The three-storey structure was an imitation of the Pazhou Pagoda in Guangzhou (formerly known as Canton). The cast-iron structure was painted with a soft red and white palette, and a mint green roof at each level. The fountain would disperse elegant streams of water into the air. Guests visiting the park could enjoy watching these streams glide in different directions, reminding them of the unprecedented beauty that the gardens provided to visitors.

❊ ❊ ❊

In the same fateful year of 1852, the Sixteenth Earl of Shrewsbury also died, leaving the estate to his cousin, Bertram, who became the Seventeenth Earl of Shrewsbury. However, the Seventeenth Earl tragically died in 1856 at the early age of twenty-four.

After the death of the Seventeenth Earl in 1856, Alton Towers was then to become locked in a ferocious legal battle over the rights to the estate and Earldom, which would last for over 3 years.

The champion of this epic battle was Henry Chetwynd-Talbot, named the Eighteenth Earl of Shrewsbury and, by the judgement of an English court of law (though contradictory to the Seventeenth Earl's will), the rightful owner of the Alton Towers estate. Unfortunately, the legal battle over the rights to Alton Towers was both long and expensive.

In 1857, as the contents of the Towers were not contested by Henry Chetwynd-Talbot, Alton Towers held a humongous sale to raise capital for their owner, the son of the Duke of Norfolk. This tragically left the Towers empty, and they would never again reach the same prestige in their decorative style.

❊ ❊ ❊

During the 1890s, the Twentieth Earl, Charles Chetwynd-Talbot, held summer fetes at Alton Towers, to set up a successful tourist attraction on the estate. This was nothing new. The Eighteenth Earl, Henry Chetwynd-Talbot, had opened the gardens of Alton Towers to the public to raise funds for restoration works. These restoration funds helped to restore many parts of the Towers that had been in decline after the legal battle that had not ended until 1860.

These summer fêtes attracted flocks of visitors to the Towers and proved how its location in the striking midlands countryside, at the very heart of England, was perfect for tourism. However, this did not change the fact that Alton Towers never truly regained its original splendour after the great sale of 1857. From this point onwards, the Shrewsbury family slowly became disengaged with the Towers, leaving it in a state of disrepair and with no interest in the estate at all.

* * *

Little occurred to Alton Towers until 1924, when John Chetwynd-Talbot, Twenty-First Earl of Shrewsbury finally sold the Towers estate to a group of local businessmen, who formed Alton Towers Ltd.

During World War II, the grounds were taken over by the War Office, for the use of training Army Cadets. When World War II ended in 1945, it is believed that the War Office was slow in returning Alton Towers to Alton Towers Ltd., but by 1952 when the estate had been returned, the owners of Alton Towers demolished many parts of the interior of Alton Towers for their valuable metals, which were in short supply after World War II.

Then, throughout the 1960s and 1970s, the park gained popularity as a funfair, with the now Towers ruins (with thanks to the businessmen who had sold many of the materials that had kept the Towers structurally sound), a boating lake and the gardens as attractions. However, it would not be until property developer John Broome took over the park that Alton Towers would begin a new journey, one that would lead to the development of Britain's most popular theme park...

PART II: ALTON TOWERS THROUGH THE DECADES

CHAPTER FOUR: FROM CORKSCREW TO BRITANNIA FARM (1980-1989)

After John Broome bought the majority share in Alton Towers Ltd. in 1973, he began to add minor attractions to the park. At this point, Alton Towers was home to a pleasant Garden, the Towers ruins, and a small funfair. However, Broome had bigger plans for Alton Towers...

In 1980, Alton Towers was to change the UK theme park industry forever, with the addition of Corkscrew. The Corkscrew would become the signature attraction at Alton Towers, the iconic double corkscrew spearheading the logo used in their TV Adverts until 1991. The ride was the first full-circuit Rollercoaster to feature 2 inversions in the United Kingdom and was an instant success.

The ride itself, compared to modern Rollercoasters, had a simple layout. Corkscrew climbed a 75 ft. lift hill, and then the ride would complete a series of banks, airtime hills, and two consecutive inversions. However, in 1980, there was no Rollercoaster in the UK like it. The story goes that on the opening day of Corkscrew, the queue to even get into the theme park stretched for hours down the winding Staffordshire country lanes- as so many were so determined to see this steel monstrosity for themselves.

The success of Corkscrew was clear in the park's attendance figures, too. In 1979, Alton Towers attracted 500,000 visitors. In 1980, with the success of the iconic Corkscrew, the park enticed over 1,000,000 visitors to the park, more than doubling the park's attendance figures in just one year.

With the success of the Corkscrew (along with a few other minor attractions, such as a Pirate Ship and an Alpine Bob Sled) in 1980, Broome started considering how he may expand the park to ensure that Alton Towers would remain the most popular theme park in the United Kingdom. Hence, in the following years, Alton Towers expanded their offerings, so that Alton Towers began to change from a grand Stately Home to an American-style theme park, in many ways like the Disney theme parks.

* * *

In 1981, Broome added a dark ride (Around the World In 80 Days), a Log Flume, a Water Show, and a Haunted House attraction to the park. In 1982, a small kiddie coaster, a kids' play area, and a 360° Cinema. 1984 brought the Black Hole coaster, and five new flat rides (Enterprise, Wave Swinger, Magic Carpet, Octopus and Turbo Star). This high investment strategy paid off, which was clear as the park's attendance was estimated to have doubled again to around 2,000,000 by 1984.

Headlining the 1981 season, The Log Flume (originally called the Wild Water Flume Ride) installed by Alton

Towers was the longest in the world. The Log Flume was to last for around six minutes and winded through the peaceful Alton Towers woodland. At an impressive 2,907 feet long, the Mack Rides log flume would be a testament to Alton Towers' ambition to become one of the top theme parks in the world.

The Log Flume would remain the same until the 1984 season, when the ride became part of the new Aqualand section of the park. This change would also see the introduction of dinosaurs to the ride as theming. Instead of a calming log flume trip through a reclusive wood, riders would now experience multiple dinosaur encounters on The Log Flume, complete with special dinosaur sound effects. The Log Flume would be the first ride at Alton Towers to offer on-ride photos. Although in the early days of the park, photos were developed and then sent to customers by mail a few days after their visit.

✳ ✳ ✳

The park would add a second major ride in 1984, with the addition of the Black Hole coaster. The ride was themed around space travel and took place in complete darkness, save for a few lighting effects. The Black Hole was a Schwarzkopf Jet Star II model, known for their dynamic turns and being able to navigate some of the tightest angles. Added to the fact that riders could not see where they were going in the darkness, the ride became notorious for being one of the sharpest turning and fastest rides in the park.

Black Hole lasted for 1 minute 50 seconds. With just shy

of 2000 ft. of track, the rollercoaster was one of the most intense rides in the park. The fact that the ride took place in the darkness made Black Hole feel much faster and more unpredictable than it was. The Black Hole was a tremendous success for Alton Towers. Featuring on-ride photos, still a very advanced concept in theme parks of the time, riding Black Hole became something of a rite of passage for young people in 1980s Britain.

The £2 Million ride was thrown into infamy, however, on 24 April 1984, after five children were injured on The Black Hole. Sensationalised reports told of The Black Hole derailing from the track, leading to serious injuries for riders. The details surrounding the reason for the crash were not made clear by Alton Towers, but an account by one of the injured riders tells of the fact that "There was some malfunction of the car which brought it to a shuddering stop… the other cars automatically came to a halt".

In reality, the scene described by riders is more telling of a failure of a guidance wheel when trying to connect with the track, or one of the ride's mechanisms (designed to make sure that the train and track are fully engaged) becoming disconnected in some manner, with the ride decelerating rapidly because of this fault.

✳ ✳ ✳

At the end of 1987, German mining firm BHS changed the Black Hole's track so that it could support the use of coupled trains. At the start of the 1988 season, the Black Hole reopened as Black Hole II. After the ride was renamed, many guests were disappointed to discover that the ride had not been re-themed and simply had a new track.

For the 1989 season, the park then renamed Black Hole II to New Black Hole. Again, very few changes were made to the Black Hole, Alton Towers had simply renamed the ride. The ride's name was later reverted back to the Black Hole.

❋ ❋ ❋

1988 would bring two new rides to the park, known as Alton Beast and Alton Mouse. The rides would join 4-Man Bob in the Talbot Street section of the park.

Anton Schwarzkopf designed Alton Beast and was a JetStar III (also known as Jumbo Jet) rollercoaster, making it the more modern version of The Black Hole ride. The ride would feature in Talbot Street, with the area dubbed 'Coaster Corner' by guests. Alton Beast was slightly faster and more intense than The Black Hole. With a speed of 44 mph and 2,862 ft. of track, the ride was in many ways like its space-themed rival in Fantasy World.

Alton Mouse also opened in 1988, a Vekoma Wild Mouse ride. Alton Mouse featured all the typical elements of a Wild Mouse coaster, tight twists and fast turns combined with the exciting but dangerous feeling which these rides are known for. The ride is reported to be the only model ever built by Vekoma, technically making the Alton Mouse the first custom ride to open at Alton Towers.

* * *

From this point, until the sale of the park in 1990, the park experienced no changes of actual importance as Broome's priorities shifted towards the construction works at Battersea that began in 1988.

John Broome's interests as a property developer meant that he always had other projects to consider. Broome boldly stated that his next project, the Battersea Power Station, would open as a leisure attraction at 2:30 pm on 21st May 1990, telling the country "Don't come at 2:35 pm or you'll miss it". The project was doomed from the very beginning- the only thing more unrealistic than the schedule for a project of this size was the budget.

By 1990, Broome had a more realistic plan for Battersea Power Station- to develop a 1000 room hotel, 1.5 million square feet of office space, and a retail outlet in the historic building. However, where would Broome get the money from to fund this project? Through the sale of Alton Towers, bringing about the end of the Broome era at Alton Towers, and allowing a new decade to bring innovative ideas and revolutionary new rides...

In his autobiography, the iconic rollercoaster designer John Wardley notes that the late 1980s appeared to him to be a poor time for Alton Towers: "It was apparent that Alton Towers was being drained of resources as a result [of the failing Battersea Project], and things seemed to be in a decline there too".

Wardley was correct to a great extent. However, this should not be misinterpreted. Although Alton Towers may have seen a slowdown in investment during its final few years under the tenure of Broome, the 1980s still brought some hugely important changes to the park: the development of Towers Street, the iconic Corkscrew and Black Hole rides and the fantastic Grand Canyon Rapids. All of these changes helped to pave the way for the park we see today and are equally important as any developments to the park seen in the 1990s.

✳ ✳ ✳

1989 brought Britannia Farm to the park, the last addition to the park under John Broome at Alton Towers. Britannia Farm was opened by The Duke of Edinburgh for the 1989 season. The new area featured a small boat ride, two shops and a milking parlour- where guests could experience farm life by milking cows.

Britannia Farm was also home to a collection of Ducks, Goats, Turkeys, Red Deer, Cattle, Pigs and Sheep. The area would see outstanding success with children and helped Alton Towers to continue to grow over the next few years.

CHAPTER FIVE: FROM THUNDER LOOPER TO OBLIVION (1990-1999)

For Alton Towers, 1990 marked an especially important year in the park's history. It was in this year that Tussauds purchased Alton Towers from John Broome, with 1990 also being year that sparked a spiral of intense development by the company in what many believe to be the golden era of Alton Towers.

Thunder Looper opened at the park in 1990 and was the first rollercoaster in the park to rival that of the Alton Towers classic, Corkscrew. Thunder looper was a Schwarzkopf shuttle coaster, having previously operated at two other theme parks in the United States. The ride was faster and considerably taller than Corkscrew, standing proud at an impressive 137.8 ft., and with a top speed of 53mph (Corkscrew, by comparison, had a top speed of 40 mph and a height of 75 ft.).

❋ ❋ ❋

This was only the beginning for Tussauds, though. The company had only just bought the park when they began to develop plans for the 1992 season. Assisted by the brilliant John Wardley, who had successfully saved the failing Chessington Zoo (now Chessington World of Adventures), Tussauds had huge ambition for what was to come in just two years...

The new team behind Alton Towers' development got to work, and it was decided that the new attractions were to be a dark ride, a new powered coaster ride and a re-theme of the area where the Grand Canyon Rapids ride could be found. The dark ride was simply named Haunted House, but many a theme park enthusiast will tell you that this dark ride was anything but conventional.

The Haunted House was to open in 1992, and the theming design was to be led by John Wardley's creative development team. The ride itself would be the largest dark ride in Europe and would feature one of the most advanced ride transit systems in the world, designed by the German company Mack Rides. Mostly because of Wardley's own experiences on a Ghost Train as a child, he was insistent that riders of this ghost train should feel alone while venturing around the Haunted House, he did not want people to feel as though they were part of "an endless procession of people in front and behind simply looking at the same thing as them".

The solution was to incorporate the best of both worlds. The ride would feature the advantages of an endless transport system, with a continuous flow of riders entering and exiting the ride. This ensured that the ride could handle many of guests and still provide the feeling of being truly alone in the Haunted House. With each carriage separating from another as the ride begins, The Haunted House feels as though every effect that riders experience is happening personally to you.

The other attraction to open in 1992 was the Runaway Mine Train, in the newly themed Katanga Canyon, resembling a peaceful African village. The area featured a new pathway that gave a much more exciting view of the also re-themed Congo River Rapids (formerly Grand Canyon Rapids). The Runaway Mine Train features interaction with the Congo River Rapids, with the two rides passing in the tunnel but in opposite directions, allowing riders to cheer and wave to one another.

✳ ✳ ✳

After the success of the 1992 season, it was time for Wardley and his team to look forwards to the park's next big Rollercoaster once again. Due to local planning restrictions on the site, rides at Alton Towers may not pass above the height of the treeline and must not be visible from the outside of the park. It seemed obvious that Wardley and his team must instead dig down.

The first plan drawn up to fill the great hole that the team intended to fill was an Arrow Pipeline coaster. The coaster was reminiscent of a bullet or missile. The intended theme was to be around a sinister military facility where something malevolent was secretly being developed. This led Wardley and his team to codename the attraction "The Secret Weapon", with the first plan being given the name "SW1", short for Secret Weapon 1. Wardley went out to Utah, U.S.A. to ride the Arrow Dynamics prototype but did not find the ride to be suitable for the park. "it was immediately apparent that this wasn't the ride for us" he remarked, "It was slow, cumbersome and boring".

Some members of the team were insistent that the Arrow Pipeline Coaster should be the new ride that Alton Towers built, and that another ride layout should be tried. A new, longer ride layout was constructed, given the name "SW2".

However, a new ride layout would not change the fact that the Pipeline coaster was a terrible ride. Just like its predecessor, the ride concept was just as dull and therefore the Arrow Pipeline concept was abandoned by Alton Towers.

At this point, Wardley had heard of a Swiss Rollercoaster firm named Bolliger & Mabillard that was developing a new type of Rollercoaster in secret, perhaps not dissimilar to the facility that the Alton Towers creative team had in mind for Secret Weapon 1. After Wardley and Nick Varney (Marketing Director of Alton Towers under Tussauds) experienced the coaster, they were convinced that this ride was a must-have for Alton Towers. This new coaster model (suspended with inversions) was decided upon and eventually named Nemesis. The theme of Nemesis was to be very original and iconic and is one of the best-themed coasters of all time.

The story goes that Nemesis comes from another dimension, millions of years ago. Wherever it went in the galaxy, it could not find a home. The Nemesis monster was feared and hated by all races it met. Two million years ago, Nemesis found refuge on Earth and rested underground – finally finding peace. Until now…

Workmen at Alton Towers were drawn, by a mysterious

force, to the place where Nemesis lay to rest. They were compelled by this force to dig until they discovered what lay beneath... Nemesis! Furious at having its home disturbed, it threw the ground above into upheaval, forming the pit which can be seen today. A secret department then came to the park, intending to pin down the creature. The steel used to pin down the creature formed the supports for the track that guests now ride upon today.

While Corkscrew may have captured the British public's attention because there was no other ride quite like it in the UK, Nemesis captured the British public's attention for an entirely different reason: not only was Nemesis a record-breaking rollercoaster for all of Europe but featured perhaps one of the most immersive backstories of any rollercoaster to mind. While some may consider the story to be somewhat lost on many of its riders today, with the original Nemesis comic no longer available for sale and the ride now featuring the Nemesis composition exclusively, the impression of racing around Nemesis' thrilling circuit in the monster's deadly lair makes Nemesis one of the most iconic coasters in all of Britain.

When comparing Nemesis to the two other major rollercoasters to open in 1994 (Shockwave at Drayton Manor and The Big One at Blackpool Pleasure Beach), Wardley points out that Nemesis features more of a theatrical experience than either Shockwave or The Big One offer. With the backstory, the stunning music composed by Graham Smart, and the beautifully landscaped surroundings, Nemesis offers one of the most memorable ride experiences to riders.

"This is the site of Nemesis- the ride. Now for the technically minded, it is a multi inversion sus- pended rollercoaster. But for the rest of you, it's just designed to scare you sh*tless!"

- JOHN WARDLEY

* * *

In 1996, Alton Towers then expanded its offerings by developing on-site accommodation, becoming Alton Towers Resort. The Alton Towers Hotel features a dynamic explorer theme, with a mix of Jules Verne-style decorations and vestiges from the many exotic places visited by the explorer who has made the Alton Towers Hotel his home.

The hotel opened to an incredibly positive reception and featured a Restaurant, Bar and Conference suite. However, the park's ambitions for on-site accommodation were far from fulfilled, with the Alton Towers Hotel showing that Alton Towers had no intention of slowing its pace, as it continues to innovate and expand its horizons.

* * *

The 1997 season would bring about the removal of Thun- der Looper. The ride had lasted only seven years at the park. Temporary planning consent had meant that its re- moval was always inevitable.

Thunder Looper would be replaced by the Ripsaw flat ride, a HUSS Topspin. Ripsaw would function as a kind of addition to the Nemesis story, with Ripsaw and The Blade (previously The Pirate Ship) said to be the tools used during the excavation of the Nemesis site.

Despite opening two new rides in 1997, attendance figures at the park had fallen by 10.3%, from 3,011,000 in 1994 (following the opening of Nemesis) to 2,700,000 in 1997. Therefore, it was clear that the park needed a new ride- a great rollercoaster to captivate the British public and make sure that Alton Towers held its place as Britain's number one theme park.

❃ ❃ ❃

After the success of Nemesis in 1994, it seemed likely that Tussauds would develop another ride with Bolliger and Mabillard in the future. By this time, the park's ambitions had reached a new level. Alton Towers had some of the best rides in all the UK, and some of the most iconic rollercoasters in all of Europe, but this was not enough. Instead, Alton Towers were planning something enormous, their first world-record beating Rollercoaster. They wanted their guests to fall into infinite darkness, to hang over the edge and fall into Oblivion…

Thus it was then, that in 1997 Alton Towers dug a great hole in Fantasy World (soon to be re-themed to X-Sector to coincide with the opening of Oblivion), with this immense hole coming to a ludicrous cost of £6 Million before a penny had even been spent on the ride, theming or advertising. Instead of announcing the ride's world-first element, the park chose instead to shroud the construction site with secrecy, asking guests to clear the area. The secretive nature of the construction of Oblivion built a kind of mystery around the ride before it had even opened.

The first hint to the public of what was to come was dropped in late 1997, in the form of a Christmas Card. The card portrayed Father Christmas diving vertically downwards, as Rudolph wanted to know what Alton Towers' new ride is going to be like.

By the start of the 1998 season, the secrecy surrounding Oblivion was truly gone- now quite the opposite. The ride's logo featured on everything from packets of Kellog's Cornflakes to deodorant cans. Within the two weeks before opening, when the world's first element was announced, Oblivion's shroud of secrecy was replaced with prominence in almost every aspect of British people's lives. Even the news channels could not get enough of Oblivion.

The ride opened to a positive reception by guests. It was not enough to beat 1994 attendance figures, but the opening of Oblivion helped to entice over 2.7 Million guests to the park in 1998, a very formidable figure indeed. At just 1 minute 15 seconds long, Oblivion always felt like quite a quick ride to many visitors. The ride was enjoyable, but frustrating considering the large build-up to the ride. It is generally accepted that Oblivion was certainly a hit for the park, but perhaps had not had as much of an impact as Nemesis, with the park even suggesting that Nemesis was their headline attraction in the 2005 Rita: Queen of Speed advert- "You said nothing could top Nemesis, not even

Oblivion..."

At this point rollercoaster fans will point out that Oblivion is not, as it was marketed to be, "The world's first vertical drop Rollercoaster". The drop was just shy of this at 87.5°. However, at the time of opening, the ride held the record for the steepest drop on a Rollercoaster in the world, meaning that even though the drop is not, in fact, truly vertical, Oblivion is still a world-record Rollercoaster. On top of this, Oblivion is also a world's first coaster specifically, even if not in the way that Alton Towers had marketed it to be. Oblivion holds the record for the world's first dive coaster.

The opening of Oblivion in 1998 marked the end of the 90s, the revolutionary decade within the park which saw Alton Towers become Alton Towers Resort, change from the ownership of Broome to the Tussauds Group, and open two of the most iconic Rollercoasters in all of Britain. However, the next decade would be equally dynamic for the park, as Wardley and his team set sights on new projects as the park continued to grow...

CHAPTER SIX: FROM HEX- THE LEGEND OF THE TOWERS TO SHARKBAIT REEF (2000-2009)

Alton Towers had begun to brainstorm for its next project, set for the year 2000. However, first, they had to deal with a big problem: Alton Towers had to pay millions in the upkeep of the Towers themselves, yet they could not do anything with it. A ride could not be placed inside the Towers themselves due to local planning restrictions, and many areas of the Towers were derelict and could not be accessed by visitors. How then could Alton Towers justify the enormous cost of restoration of the many parts of the Towers that needed attention if they could not place an attraction in the Towers when these works were complete?

The solution was to place a queue line and pre-show within the newly restored area of the Towers, which could be removed without leaving any lasting impact upon this Grade II listed building, and place the new attraction itself within a temporary shelter outside of the Towers so that no parts of the Towers (and the beautiful legacy that they portray) would be impacted by the ride's life. With a location within the park in mind, the park's development team decided upon a Vekoma Mad House attraction and had the idea that since the ride was to be completed as part of a restoration project within the park, the team would theme the ride accordingly, with a local legend taking centre place as the theme of the ride.

Hex: Legend of the Towers tells the legend of the chained oak. The chained oak exists in real life beyond the fictional Hex storyline. In fact, the tree can still be visited today, with directions easily accessible online.

* * *

The chained oak lies down an old and shaded forest path. The steep downwards gradient and the thick woodland give a real sense of adventure as you head down towards the site where the tree lies.

When you reach the tree, you find old stone steps winding closer to the chained oak itself, almost daring you to come closer. The oak itself is magnificent, the chains suppressing it remain firmly in place hundreds of years on, almost warning of the dangers that the tree poses. Although it seems unlikely that the tree is truly cursed as the legend states, the area where the tree stands seems shrouded in an eerie, cryptic feeling- no wonder that the story suited the ride so well...

* * *

The legend goes that the Fifteenth Earl of Shrewsbury was

travelling back to his home, Alton Towers when an old beggar woman appeared by the roadside. She asked for a coin, but the Earl dismissed her and continued upon his journey. The beggar screamed a curse upon the Earl "for every branch of the old oak tree that falls, a member of your family will die". Later that fateful night, a branch of the old oak tree fell in a storm. Also, that very night, a member of the Earl's family suddenly, and mysteriously, died. Now believing in the curse, the Earl ordered the tree to be chained up to prevent any further deaths.

In Hex: Legend of the Towers, the story is then continued- telling how the Earl then dragged the fallen branch back to Alton Towers and sealed the branch in a vault, attempting to conduct experiments on the branch in a battle of Science against The Supernatural. This part extends the legend, but provides the exciting backstory to the vault within the Towers which visitors explore in the ride, the vault in which the Mad House attraction itself is situated.

The ride experience itself involves visitors entering the vault in which the tree lies. Seated, they then experience a swinging motion as they begin to sway from side to side. At the same time, the room itself moves, giving riders the sensation of being upside down, when the ride only tilts riders around 15° in either direction. Hex- The Legend of the Towers may have been a less conventional attraction in comparison to the other commanding rollercoasters of Alton Towers, but the ride's authentic theme makes it a real gem for visitors, many leaving the attraction wondering how much of the legend is real, and with a little more appreciation for the historic Towers and the great story which lies behind them…

* * *

After the opening of Oblivion in 1998, Tussauds had immediately made it clear to John Wardley and his team that the next big rollercoaster at Alton Towers, Secret Weapon 5, needed to be another "world's first" coaster for the park. While developing Hex, which would open in the year 2000, Alton Towers was already far into planning this next Secret Weapon.

Turning again to Bolliger & Mabillard, the park again decided that they wanted to develop another new type of coaster experience. This time, the ride experience was to be something much smoother and calmer than any other type of ride in the world- the flying coaster.

In some respect, the title of the world's first flying coaster had already been taken. Skytrak opened in 1997, at Granada Studios in Manchester. However, the ride was plagued with technical difficulties and only opened at the very end of the 1997 season and the start of the 1998 season, before closing permanently. The ride itself featured an odd loading system, with riders climbing a sort of ladder to enter the harness, before being locked into a small cage.

While Skytrak was a step in the right direction, the ride technology left a lot to be desired. The ride had a very low capacity of 240 riders per hour, although for a much smaller park like Granada Studios, this would have made very little impact on queue times.

The next attempt at a flying coaster was by Vekoma, with

Stealth opening at California's Great America in Santa Clara, California, on 1 April 2000. Stealth featured an improvement on the loading system used on Skytrak, with riders seated backwards when sitting down on the ride, then lowered to face the ceiling with their backs facing the track. Riders would then ascend a lift hill before the track would flip riders into a flying position, experiencing 5 inversions before the ride placed visitors onto their backs once more. While the Stealth loading system was more efficient than Skytrak's, featuring a far higher capacity of 1,000 riders per hour, the awkward nature of riders being placed on their backs and then flipped was something to be improved when Secret Weapon 6 opened in 2002. The ride operated at the park for just three years, before being moved to Carowinds in North Carolina.

Back at Alton Towers, plans were being created for the theming of this new flying coaster. Secret Weapon 6, later to be known as Air, would have riders seated in a position similar to that of a suspended coaster such as Nemesis, with two small restraints holding the riders' lower legs in place and a soft padded over-the-shoulder harness to ensure that riders are both supported and comfortable when riding Air. Guests would then be raised into a flying position, with their backs facing the track and heads facing forwards.

Sponsored by Cadbury Heroes, the iconic British chocolate confectionery, Air opened in 2002 to a very positive response. Although both Skytrak and Stealth had operated before Air, the ride was the first B&M flying coaster in the world, arguably far more advanced to its flying coaster predecessors. Thanks to its dual-bay loading system, the ride opened with an enormous rider capacity of 1,500 riders per hour. The ride's loading system was a game-changer, being far more comfortable than Skytrak or Stealth, with Air providing a far more calming flying experience than Stealth and a freer flying sensation than Skytrak.

The ride was unlike anything else found in the UK, and so not only helped to expand Alton Towers' offerings as a theme park but helped to keep Alton Towers as the most popular theme park in the UK. Air opened to great popularity within the park, and to this day remains one of the park's most popular rides, offering an experience unlike any other ride in the park...

After the opening of Air in 2002, Alton Towers had decided that John Wardley would be replaced by a new creative director, namely Candy Holland. Wardley seemed perfectly happy with this and considered himself retired.

* * *

The next major instalment for the park came in 2003, with the opening of the Splash Landings Hotel. Themed extensively around a Caribbean getaway, with the Ma Garrita's bar, Flambo's restaurant and rooms designed to further involve guests in this theme, the park again continued with its theme of escapism (now a coined term by the park) with the Splash Landings Hotel. The colourful tropical paradise theme gave the hotel a notable contrast from the gloomy British weather outside on bitterly cold days, with Splash Landings enjoying similar success to its neighbouring hotel, the Alton Towers Hotel.

※ ※ ※

In 2004, the park opened Spinball Whizzer. The ride was a
Maurer Rides SC2200 Spinning Coaster and offers a 'pink-
knuckle' ride experience, meaning that the ride is enjoyable for young people and older riders alike. While the ride
may not be as intense as other major rollercoasters, such
as Nemesis or Oblivion, it offers a thrilling experience for
riders, with 1 minute 15 seconds of dizziness and disorien-
tation for riders as Spinball Whizzer navigates the many
banks and helices the ride takes.

N.B: From 2010 to 2015, Spinball Whizzer would be re-
themed to Sonic Spinball, after entering a licensing agree-
ment with games publisher SEGA® to use characters from
the Sonic the Hedgehog™ games as part of the theme of the
ride. In 2016, Sonic Spinball would return to the original
Spinball Whizzer theme after the park's license to use the
SEGA® theme was not renewed.

※ ※ ※

By the start of the 2004 season, The Log Flume had been
rebranded. Receiving a sponsorship with soap manufacturer Imperial Leather, the ride became known as The
Flume. The ride now featured bright red bathtubs as
trains, with assorted duck theming scattered about the
ride.

After a series of small lifts and drops, the ride slowly
climbs another small lift. From here, riders would tumble

down another water chute. However, guests now found themselves in complete darkness. The ride then featured a small duck, which watches you on the edge of a bathtub as you pass. The Flume then returned into blackness as riders then continue to navigate the twists and turns of The Flume, before reaching the scariest part of the ride- the jump scare.

The lights flicker on. This reveals the colossal duck towering over you, quacking maliciously, before The Flume scrambles away from the terrifying duck and back to the safety of the outside world. In the dark, this duck is undoubtedly the scariest element of The Flume, even in a comical sense. After this horrifying encounter, guests clamber up a slow lift hill, giving them time to recover from the horrors of The Flume's indoor section, before tumbling down the ride's finale, an 85 ft. splashdown into the reservoir below.

※ ※ ※

Then, in 2005, came the opening of another major rollercoaster for the park. Although this ride would not be a Secret Weapon like Nemesis or Air, this would not stop the park from billing the ride as "your best Alton Towers ride ever" during adverts for the 2005 season. Rita is still a major ride for the park, though, featuring as one of the major six rollercoasters for the park's 2015 "Big Six Challenge".

Rita featured a launch of 0-61.1 mph in just 2.5 seconds. This made Rita a relatively fast ride for the park, although coaster enthusiasts pointed out that the top speed on this

Intamin Accelerator Coaster was slower than the drop on Oblivion. The ride was ludicrously short at just 25 seconds long (even Oblivion was 1 minute 15 seconds long) and has received extremely mixed reviews ever since.

Fans of the ride often point out that the ride was the first hydraulic launch coaster in Europe, and how Rita helped to diversify the park's offerings with a ride of sheer speed and thrill. Opponents to the ride, however, point out that it was poorly themed (Rita was themed around drag racing, which did not compliment the themes of Ug Land or the Dark Forest) and rushed after the park failed to gain planning permission to open a wooden coaster in the park for the 2005 season.

❋ ❋ ❋

In 2005, Dubai International Capital purchased the Tussauds Group for £800 Million.

Dubai International Capital would then sell the Tussauds Group to Merlin Entertainments (who, at the time, owned just a handful of minor attractions including Legoland parks and Sea Life Centres) for £1 Billion in 2007. It was at this point in 2007 when John Wardley was asked to return to work for the Tussauds Group and Alton Towers as a consultant, a role that would see him involved in the development of the park's next big coaster...

❋ ❋ ❋

In 2009, though, the park's owners Merlin decided that

they would promote one of their other types of attraction, a Sea Life Centre, within the park. The attraction operated at no additional cost to visitors. The centre, named Sharkbait Reef, opened at a cost of £4 Million in 2009. The Sea Life Centre has a pirate theme to match the surrounding Mutiny Bay area and features over 1 million litres of water, with more than 300 different species of fish.

CHAPTER SEVEN: FROM TH13TEEN TO THE ALTON TOWERS DUNGEON (2010-2019)

After Wardley's return in 2007, the park's creative team developed ideas for the park's next big coaster. The iconic Corkscrew rollercoaster had closed in 2008, and with plans for its replacement to open in 2010, the park needed something big- something that could live up to the name of deserving to replace Corkscrew.

Secret Weapon 6 would be the park's first rollercoaster in the Secret Weapon series not to be built by Bolliger & Mabillard (excluding Secret Weapons 1 and 2, which were never built). Secret Weapon 6, which would become known as Th13teen, would be built by Bolliger & Mabillard's rival Intamin, who had built Rita: Queen of Speed just metres away from Th13teen five years earlier.

Similar to the opening of Oblivion, the unique element of Th13teen was kept secret throughout design and construction, until just a few weeks before the opening of Th13teen the world's first element was announced, a revolutionary idea for a coaster, and one that completely changed what people thought rollercoasters were capable of...

Th13teen - The world's first freefall drop rollercoaster

Intamin had achieved what was previously thought to be impossible. Past rides had tilted the track while riders were on it so that riders could navigate a section of a track before the ride tilted and riders could navigate the same track backwards (or slowly point riders downwards into a vertical drop, like Gravity Max at Discovery World Taiwan), but Th13teen would feature a drop unlike any other in the world.

Unlike tilt coasters, Th13teen would feature the track itself falling vertically, with riders facing forwards during the drop. The sensation of a freefall drop was unlike any other in the world, but Alton Towers knew that the ride would easily be copied within a matter of years, so the creative team made sure that Th13teen would stay as not only the first but the best version in the world.

After navigating a short circuit of twists and helices typical of any family coaster, Th13teen climbs a short Booster Wheel Lift Hill towards a small crypt. Riders are engulfed in darkness, with only small torches in the mysterious crypt as the entrance door to the crypt closes, leaving riders in almost complete darkness. The sound of creaking wood surrounds you, alerting riders that the foundations of the crypt may not be as sturdy as one would hope. Then, the torches flicker into blackness and the train jolts in the darkness. Guests unbeknownst to the ride's secret are then caught off-guard, believing the ride to be over, as Th13teen then plunges downwards 5 metres (16.4 ft.) in complete darkness. The eyes of the ominous figures which haunt the Dark Forest then light up as Th13 teen then plunges riders backwards through a dark tunnel, before re-emerging just outside of the ride's station.

When Th13teen opened in 2010, the Ug Land area would be re-themed to the Dark Forest, telling the story of how a mysterious force had taken over the forest, making the entire area cursed. The adverts for Alton Towers in 2010 came with a menacing notice to potential visitors of the park, warning them of what lies in wait in the Dark Forest: "If you go down to the woods today... You better not go alone..."

To make the ride better suit the area, Rita: Queen of Speed was renamed to Rita, with the theme of the ride shifting from drag racing to a much darker theme of escaping the Dark Forest. This time, the riders of Rita were survivors of the forest's wrath and were now desperately trying to escape the Dark Forest.

A theory amongst some Alton Towers fans is that Th13teen is an extension of the Hex: Legend of the Towers theme. In some ways, the forest themes and curse/myth themes of the two rides seem similar, with a dark antagonistic force taking front in both rides' stories. The parallels between the two rides are interesting, however there is very little evidence from Alton Towers to suggest that the two rides are in any way linked- perhaps the proximity of Hex: Legend of the Towers to Th13teen influenced the designers' ideas for the theming of Th13teen in some manner...

After expanding their offerings to thrill-seekers in 2010, the park again looked to add another intense attraction in 2012. During years of important national events, such as Royal Weddings or World Cup Finals, theme parks often experience slightly lower attendance figures because of alternative national events effectively "stealing the scene" from the big theme parks. Therefore when it was announced that London would host the 2012 Olympics, it seemed clear that Merlin would need something new and exciting to draw the British population's attention away from the Olympics and make sure that a trip to Alton Towers would be at the forefront of the nations' mind for the glorious summer of 2012.

In response to the upcoming 2012 London Olympics, Merlin added the brilliant Bolliger & Mabillard wing coaster The Swarm to Thorpe Park in 2012. Chessington World of Adventures received a new live show, plus a newly themed African section of the park. In 2012, Alton Towers tapped into an existing part of the park's reputation, with a continuation of the Nemesis storyline...

* * *

Headlining the 2012 season for the park, Nemesis Sub-Terra extended the Nemesis storyline, with the Phalanx (the company in charge of monitoring the Nemesis site) inviting riders to observe the newly found Nemesis egg in a chamber deep underground. The ride featured an ABC

Rides Freefall Tower, like the drop towers used on Merlin's Blackpool Dungeon and London Dungeon attractions.

After being invited to visit the egg, guests are 'briefed' about the Nemesis Sub-Terra site by the onsite military staff, the Phalanx. This briefing, or pre-show, involved visitors being warned of the dangers of what lay beneath them. Guests are then 'sent down' to visit the chamber via a lift. Once underground, guests are seated in the observation chamber (with lap bars), arranged in four inwards-facing rows of ten seats. There is a power failure, and Nemesis Sub-Terra then falls a further 6 metres (20 feet) downwards in the darkness.

This leaves riders in a secondary chamber which is unsecure and not safe for visitors. The lights flicker on, and the hatched Nemesis eggs were revealed to riders. Here, a mix of water effects and air bursts were used to imitate the Nemesis creature moving around the cavern. Then, riders were once more engulfed in darkness and began to climb back up to the original chamber as the power had been restored.

Upon returning to the original chamber, Phalanx operatives then move riders into the lifts back to the surface. As guests are trying to escape, the Nemesis monster once again attacks, leaving the lift damaged. Riders then make their way through a horror maze, with live actors and strobe lighting, before making their way back into the world outside.

* * *

Nemesis Sub-Terra lasted just three years. Closing during the 2015 season after the crash of The Smiler, Nemesis Sub-Terra would not reopen for the 2016 season- indeed, the ride has not reopened since. Although no plans have been submitted to replace Nemesis Sub-Terra, a horror maze named Project 42 has been housed in the Nemesis Sub-Terra site for the 2018 and 2019 seasons, and it seems very unlikely that Nemesis Sub-Terra will ever re-open.

After Nemesis Sub-Terra had opened, rumour quickly spread about the park's next big ride. There was speculation that it would be another Secret Weapon. These rumours were correct, as Alton Towers had begun the development of something incredibly special indeed, they had begun the development of Secret Weapon 7...

* * *

In 2012, Merlin Entertainments filed for a trademark for what was likely to be the name of their next big ride. The patent was for the name The Smiler. Speculation continued as to what type of ride Secret Weapon 7 would be. Similarly to Oblivion and Th13teen, the world's first element of The Smiler was kept a secret by the park to give the ride a feeling of mystery and secrecy before the ride had even opened.

In 2013, the park would open The Smiler on the old site of the park's famous Black Hole coaster. Alton Towers had decided that Secret Weapon 7 would be the ride to beat, setting the benchmark for what Rollercoaster designers may have previously thought beyond design. The creative development team at Alton Towers hold themselves to a very high standard when developing new rides, so when Alton Towers decided that Secret Weapon 7 was going to be the one to knock Nemesis off the number one spot as the park's best ride, it hardly seems surprising that the result would be a world-beating rollercoaster unlike any other found across the globe

As construction began on the steel monstrosity that was to become known as The Smiler, speculation mounted regarding how many inversions the ride might have, as an increasing number of curved pieces of track arrived at the park. The Smiler's planning applications had been sneakily designed so that even when released to the public domain, it would be impossible to find out how many inversions the ride had.

The earlier record for the greatest number of inversions on a ride was 10, set with the opening of Colossus at sister Merlin park Thorpe Park Resort in 2002. The Smiler would feature a record-breaking 14 inversions and would attract attention from media companies all around the world. At an enormous cost of £18 Million, The Smiler would be Alton Towers' new iconic figurehead rollercoaster and would cement the park's name as one of the best theme parks in the world.

Alton Towers announced the ride's opening on the park's Twitter page on 31 May 2013. The Smiler would enjoy a level of fame rivalled only by that of the Corkscrew and Nemesis.

German firm Gerstlauer manufactured the ride, the figurehead of its Infinity Coaster range. A ride of this calibre was a great challenge for even Gerstlauer, and the ride was delayed multiple times. Because of this, The Smiler recieved bad publicity for changing its opening date last-minute multiple times, leading to customer complaints that they had to keep changing their booking dates to come and visit the park.

Despite all of this, the ride opened on 31 May 2013 and was a tremendous success. Themed as an extension to an existing story of one of the park's horror mazes, The Sanctuary, The Smiler tells the story of a sinister organisation designed to make people happy. While the Ministry of Joy almost sounds like a pleasant government department, its methods of making people happy are what gives the ride its creepy and disturbing atmosphere.

The Smiler was designed as a kind of medical procedure for people who struggled to feel happiness in their lives. Riders of The Smiler are volunteers opting to have this medical procedure to make themselves happier. The sinister aspect of the ride is slightly more subtle; the soundtrack to the ride is essentially just people laughing (although in unison, as though the laughing is a type of war cry of an army of subjects exposed to The Smiler), and the ride features nothing more than a range of colourful optical illusions (with occasional elusive glitches to remind visitors that The Smiler was not as friendly as it seemed). The ride opened, knocking Nemesis off the number one spot as the most popular ride in the park, and John Wardley retired as a consultant for Alton Towers' creative team, this time for good.

✳ ✳ ✳

After the opening of The Smiler in 2013, it seemed like nothing could stop Alton Towers. This was not true, however, and on 2 June 2015 at 13:51, the impossible happened. A train carrying 16 passengers crashed into an empty carriage after the empty carriage had stalled in between two loops on the ride. The Smiler had safeguards that prevented two carriages from occupying the same section of track, so how could the system fail?

Four trains ran that day on The Smiler. Due to a technical problem on the ride, ride engineers were called to the site. First, these ride engineers had added an extra train to The Smiler because of long waiting times for the ride. This train stalled due to high winds, during its first navigation of the day, and had to be pushed by engineers so it would re-engage with the system. A second empty train was then sent round, and again this train stalled, but at a different point in the ride. Engineers could not see the stalled carriage on the ride's CCTV cameras and handed the ride back over to the ride operators. Due to poor communication, ride operators were unaware that a fifth train had been added to The Smiler.

A full train was then sent out, holding 16 riders, and stopped on The Smiler's first lift hill. Unaware that a fifth train had been added to The Smiler's circuit, ride operators then overrode the safeguard that prevented two carriages from occupying the same section of track, believing that this was a simple computer malfunction. The train carrying 16 riders then made its way through The Smiler's circuit, before colliding with the stalled empty carriage.

As a result of the crash, Merlin Entertainments pleaded

guilty in court to breaching the Health and Safety Act and was fined £5 Million. Immediately after the incident, four rides across three Merlin theme parks were closed for inspection: The Smiler at Alton Towers, Saw: The Ride at Thorpe Park and Dragon's Fury and Rattlesnake, both at Chessington World of Adventures.

Nemesis Sub-Terra would also be closed after the incident and would be left SBNO (Standing But Not Operating) until the ride was removed from the park's official website before the start of the 2019 season, indicating that the ride is likely to have been closed permanently.

✳ ✳ ✳

In 2016, Alton Towers would try to bring visitors back to the park by re-theming Air to feature Virtual Reality (VR) goggles. Air would become known as Galactica, with the B&M Flying Coaster now themed as an opportunity for guests to explore deep space. With the ride now featuring a vast blue portal where the cameras for Air had once stood, riders were transported via Virtual Reality to explore planets such as Vega 10 or Espin.

The ride would receive a new logo, soundtrack, portal, lighting, and even the loading stations for the ride would get a re-theme, with video screens explaining the journey that passengers were about to take.

Also opening in 2016, the Rollercoaster Restaurant was designed to celebrate Alton Towers' history of creating some of the most iconic coasters in the world. Food at the Rollercoaster Restaurant is delivered to guests via a small, winding steel track. Galactica opened with the park's new Rollercoaster Restaurant, occupying most of the space where the old Air shop had stood.

On 17 March 2019, Alton Towers announced on their official Twitter page that Galactica would no longer feature VR headsets, due to guest feedback about their experience on Galactica with the headsets.

Even though Galactica was to lose its Virtual Reality headsets, the ride kept its space exploration theme, and Air would no longer exist.

❊ ❊ ❊

After opening Galactica in 2016, Alton Towers decided that it was time for a new Secret Weapon. However, what did the park not have when it came to world-beating rollercoasters? It had some of the fastest, loopiest, steepest, and most extreme coasters in the world. Secret Weapon 8 would take the park in a new direction.

When developing the parks' next Secret Weapon, Secret Weapon 8, the park's creative team took a gamble and chose to build a type of coaster that had an extremely poor reputation in the UK. A wooden rollercoaster. To the British public, wooden rollercoasters were rough, old, and dangerous rides- the complete antithesis of what Alton Towers strives to be.

How, then, could the park convince the public otherwise? Alton Towers closed The Flume in 2015, one of the park's oldest and most popular rides. Opening in 1981, The

Flume would last 34 years at Alton Towers. The log flume attraction had become a nostalgic staple to many theme parks, but as Alton Towers continued to modernise and update its offerings, it was decided that The Flume would not re-open as many expected for the 2016 season, with the site instead being earmarked for a new attraction, to become known as Secret Weapon 8...

For the park's 2017 Scarefest event, Alton Towers would create a horror maze designed as a prequel to the Wicker Man ride. This would be known as "The Welcoming: Be Chosen" and allowed visitors to venture through the mysterious village of the Beornen tribe, who had taken to worshipping a mysterious god of fire. The park posted hints to the ride's nature on their YouTube channel, featuring a mysterious cypher for fans to work out, to learn more details of the mysterious SW8.

The Wicker Man runes that had featured on the Secret Weapon 8 teaser videos would later be used in the Wicker Man queue line, with phrases such as 'Feed the flames' written in this mysterious code. Wicker Man merchandise would also feature these peculiar symbols, along with bunting hanging from the queue line, again emblazoned with the Wicker Man runes.

Manufactured by Great Coasters International (GCI for short), Wicker Man would open at the park in 2018, branded as the world's first ride to combine a wooden rollercoaster and fire. GCI is a U.S.-based coaster manufacturer, known for creating some of the most modern and cutting-edge Wooden Rollercoasters in the world- such as InvadR at Busch Gardens Williamsburg, and Ghostrider at Knott's Berry Farm in California.

Riders on Wicker Man journey through a winding queue line as they venture deep into the woods where the Beornen, the mysterious village who worship a kind of animal god, are said to live. The cult has invited guests to visit their home and learn more about the Beornen tribes' lives, but as soon as guests enter Wicker Man's pre-show situated in a small wooden hut, the truth emerges. You are a gift to be sacrificed to this mysterious god- and now your life is in grave danger.

Riders then enter the Wicker Man's train and traverse the circuit of dips, banks, and twists towards the towering Wicker Man effigy as the ritual begins. As the train approaches the magnificent structure, the Wicker Man erupts into flames as riders pass through the flaming body of The Wicker Man, now brought to life by the ritual. Visitors then pass through the Wicker Man twice more before the ride makes its way back towards the station, slowing down as it reaches the final brake run in a dim tunnel, special effects sending sprawling clusters of 'flames' towards you in the darkness...

With the Wicker Man soundtrack designed by IMAscore, whose music portfolio includes films such as Star Wars: The Rise Of Skywalker, video games such as Final Fantasy XV, plus atmospheric music for popular European theme parks such as Phantasialand, as well as the soundtrack for Alton Towers' Galactica ride. IMAscore created a dark and tense soundtrack for the ride, with riders surrounded by the reverberations of the Beornen's mysterious ritual as they approach the dark fate that the Wicker Man holds for visitors.

The ride itself was a momentous success for the park, ranking in 5th place for the title of Amusement Today's Golden Ticket Awards for Best New Amusement Park Ride Of 2018.

* * *

In 2019, Merlin would add another one of its 'Midway Attractions' to the park, something not as gigantic as one of its rollercoasters, but instead an intermediate level of investment into the park. This took the form of one of Merlin's Dungeons attractions, entering the park on the old site of Charlie and the Chocolate Factory: The Ride. Unlike the park's Sea Life attraction, the Alton Towers Dungeon would be a paid-for experience- although premium Merlin annual pass holders and premium Alton Towers season pass holders would be allowed free entry to the attraction. The experience would last some 45 minutes, featuring six scenes and a boat ride down the Black River.

Reception to the attraction was positive, the Dungeons were a welcome addition to the park as Alton Towers continued to expand their offerings. The Alton Towers Dungeon featured special effects, live actors, and even a small indoor ride. Although, it is interesting that after the short-lived lifespan of Nemesis Sub-Terra, the park chose not to add a 'Drop Dead' drop tower, similar to the ones used at The Blackpool Tower Dungeon and The Edinburgh Dungeon Attractions, instead opting for a boat ride attraction for the Alton Towers Dungeon.

GALLERY

A view of The Smiler from outside The Smiler Shop, as it navigates the Batwing element of the ride

The Pagoda Fountain, pictured after its 3-month restoration in 2017

A landscape view of the stunning Alton Towers ruins, pictured in 2008

A view of the iconic Corkscrew which catalysed the enormous growth of Alton Towers into the theme park that we see today.

Nemesis navigating the ride's vertical loop. Nemesis opened in 1994, as Europe's first inverted rollercoaster

A view of the fountain and lake from the Alton Towers Hotel

Sir Algenon's famous air balloon, the centrepiece of the Jules Verne-style Alton Towers Hotel

Foreground: Rita, the Intamin accelerator coaster, after the 2010 Dark Forest re-theme

Background: The mysterious and decrepit crypt of Th13 teen, housing the world's first freefall drop rollercoaster

A view of Wicker Man from the Fast Track entrance to the ride.

PART III: APPENDICES

APPENDIX I: RESOURCES

Below you will find a list of further reading and resources if you wish to explore further into the history of the Towers.

Books

Creating my own Nemesis | John Wardley | ISBN 9781484049143

Smoke & Mirrors: The Haunted House of Alton Towers | Michael P. Eley | ISBN 9781490417080

Alton Towers: A Gothic Wonderland | Michael Fisher | ISBN 0952685523

Alton Towers: Past and Present | Michael Fisher | ISBN 978-1843064091

Discovering Alton Towers | Malcolm McIntosh | ISBN 0721411266

Tales from the Towers | Nick Sim | ISBN 9781492377160

Websites

Alton Towers' official website https://www.altontowers.com/

Towers Street https://towersstreet.com/

Towers Times https://www.towerstimes.co.uk/

RollerCoasterDataBase https://rcdb.com/

YouTube Channels

Towers Times and South Parks Media

https://www.youtube.com/user/TowersTimesMedia

Alton Towers Official

https://www.youtube.com/user/officialaltontowers

Theme Park Worldwide

https://www.youtube.com/user/ThemeParkWorldwide

TheJackSilkstone

https://www.youtube.com/channel/UCKknpFhCx-WnyJc7bkPyewJg

<u>N.B</u>: The author takes no responsibility for the content of external media such as Books or Websites.

APPENDIX II: TIMELINE

716 A.D. - Battle between Kings Ceolred of Mercia and Ine of Wessex

1807- Fifteenth Earl of Shrewsbury, Charles Talbot, buys out the Burtons' share of the Alveton Estate and invests in work on the property.

1827- Charles Talbot dies, leaving the estate to John Talbot, the Sixteenth Earl of Shrewsbury. The Sixteenth Earl continues upon the same path as his predecessor, completing works on the Gardens and House, as started by his uncle.

1837- The Talbots' principal residence in Heythrop is burned down, and the family makes Alton Towers their new home permanently. Pugin first visits Alton Towers in August of this year.

1852-The Sixteenth Earl of Shrewsbury dies

1857- Henry Chetwynd-Talbot becomes the Eighteenth Earl of Shrewsbury. Later, after a long and ferocious legal battle, Henry comes into possession of the Alton Towers Estate.

1924- The Estate and House are sold to a group of locals, who form Alton Towers Ltd.

1973- John Broome buys the majority share and becomes the main shareholder of the Alton Towers company and Estate

1980- The Corkscrew rollercoaster is added to the park

1981- The Log Flume, Around the World In 80 Days and Doom & Son's attractions open

1984- Black Hole and a variety of flat rides open in the park

1986- Towers Street built, Grand Canyon Rapids open

1987- Sky Ride, Monorail and Swan Boats open

1988- The arrival of Alton Beast and Alton Mouse

1990- Thunder Looper headlines in the park's new area, Thunder Valley.

Tussauds Group purchases Alton Towers for £60 Million from John Broome.

1992- Haunted House and Runaway Mine train open

1994- Europe's first Inverted Rollercoaster, Nemesis, opens.

1996- The Theme Park becomes Alton Towers Resort, with the addition of the Alton Towers Hotel

1998- The world's first Vertical Drop Rollercoaster, Oblivion, opens, plunging riders down a 180 ft. drop

2000- Hex - The Legend of the Towers opens

2002- Air opens in Forbidden Valley, the world's first flying coaster built by the iconic Bolliger and Mabillard coaster company

2003- Alton Towers Resort adds a second hotel, Splash Landings Hotel, to the park.

The Haunted House is re-themed to Duel, adding interactive laser blasters to the ride

2004- Spinball Whizzer opens, a classic spinning coaster by German firm Maurer Rides

2005- Rita - Queen of Speed opens, capable of reaching speeds of 61.1 mph.

Dubai International Capital purchases the Tussauds Group and, hence, Alton Towers Resort

2007- Merlin Entertainments buys the Tussauds group, running the park on a 35-year lease from investment firm Prestbury.

2009- Sharkbait Reef opens to the public, costing £4 Million to construct

2010- Th13teen opens, the world's first freefall drop coaster

2012- Nemesis: Sub Terra opens, continuing the Nemesis legend at the park.

2013- The Smiler opens, the world's first '14-Looping Rollercoaster', smashing the prior record of ten inversions.

2016- Air re-themed to Galactica, the world's first Rollercoaster fully dedicated to Virtual Reality.

2018- Wicker Man opens, the first Wooden Rollercoaster to be built in the UK in over 20 years.

2019- The Alton Towers Dungeons opens

APPENDIX III: RIDE FACTS

Ride Name	Cost	Track Length	Height of Drop	Ride Duration	Top Speed	Capacity per Hour
The Smiler	£18 Million	1170 Metres	30 Metres	165 Seconds	85 Km/hr	1000 Passengers
Oblivion	£12 Million	373 Metres	60 Metres	160 Seconds	110 Km/hr	1900 Passengers
Nemesis	£10 Million	716 Metres	13 Metres	195 Seconds	81 Km/hr	1400 Passengers
Galactica	£12 Million	840 Metres	20 Metres	189 Seconds	75 Km/hr	1500 Passengers
Rita	£8 Million	647 Metres	18.4 Metres	49 Seconds	100 Km/hr	1150 Passengers
Th13teen	£15 Million	800 Metres	19 Metres	120 Seconds	68 Km/hr	1400 Passengers
Wicker Man	£16 Million	795 Metres	22 Metres	210 Seconds	70 Km/hr	952 Passengers

APPENDIX IV: REFERENCES

- Michael J. Fisher, Alton Towers: A Gothic Wonderland, 1999, p.15
- BBC News Article, Anglo-Saxon Mercia: Some Facts and Some Legends | The battle of... Alton Towers, 2011 https://www.bbc.co.uk/news/uk-england-stoke-stafford-shire-13105212
- Nick Sim, Tales from The Towers, 2013, p.13
- Unknown Author, Earl of Shrewsbury | Titleholders, 2020, https://en.wikipedia.org/wiki/Earl_of_Shrewsbury#Earls_of_Shrewsbury_Second_Creation_(1442)
- Dr Robert Plot, The Natural History of Staffordshire, 1686, p.40
- Unknown Author, Lost Heritage of Alton Towers | Alton Lodge, 2020 http://www.lostheritage.org.uk/houses/lh_staffordshire_altontowers.html
- Fisher, Alton Towers: A Gothic Wonderland, 1999, p.20
- Malcolm McIntosh, Discovering Alton Towers, 1988, p.33
- Unknown Author, History of Alton Towers, 2020, https://en.wikipedia.org/wiki/History_of_Alton_Towers
- RollerCoasterDataBase (RCDB), Rita | Alton Towers | Staffordshire | United Kingdom, 2020, https://rcdb.com/2787.htm
- Alton Towers Almanac, History | Alton Towers Timeline, 2020 http://www.towersalmanac.com/history/index.php?id=2
- Jacqueline Banerjee, The Victorian Web Home | Visual Arts | Victorian Architecture | A.W.N Pugin, 2012, http://www.victorianweb.org/art/architecture/pugin/24.html

- Unknown Author, *The Tussauds Group | The 1900s*, 2020, https://en.wikipedia.org/wiki/The_Tussauds_Group#The_1900s
- Towers Expert, *Alton Towers TV Advertisements (1980-2018)*, https://www.youtube.com/watch?v=CJdTn764nCs
- Coasterpedia, *Corkscrew (Alton Towers)*, 2020, https://coasterpedia.net/wiki/Corkscrew_(Alton_Towers)
- James Salter, *Alton Towers | Rides | Corkscrew*, 2020, https://www.themeparkjames.co.uk/theme-parks/europe/uk/alton-towers/rides/corkscrew/
- Nick Sim, *Tales from the Towers*, 2013, p.137
- Nick Sim, *Tales from the Towers*, 2013, p.138
- John Wardley, *Creating my own Nemesis*, 2015, p.132
- RollerCoasterDataBase (RCDB), *Thunder Looper | Alton Towers | Staffordshire | United Kingdom*, 2020, https://rcdb.com/798.htm
- RollerCoasterDataBase (RCDB), *Corkscrew | Alton Towers | Staffordshire | United Kingdom*, 2020, https://rcdb.com/778.htm
- Unknown Author, *Alton Towers Wiki*, 2020, https://alton-tower.fandom.com/wiki/Duel
- Michael P. Eley, *Smoke & Mirrors: The Haunted house of Alton Towers*, 2012, p.26
- John Wardley, *Creating my own Nemesis*, 2015, p.134
- John Wardley, *Creating my own Nemesis*, 2015, p.138
- Nick Sim, *Tales from the Towers*, 2013, p.178
- Matt N., *Alton Towers visitor figures through the years*, 2020, https://towersstreet.com/talk/threads/alton-towers-visitor-figures-through-the-years.4640/
- RollerCoasterDataBase (RCDB), *Oblivion | Alton Towers | Staffordshire | United Kingdom*, 2020, https://rcdb.com/777.htm

- *Towers Times, Oblivion, 2020, https://www.towerstimes.co.uk/theme-park/x-sector/oblivion/*
- *Nick Sim, Tales from the Towers, 2013, p.180*
- *Nick Sim, Tales from the Towers, 2013, p.254*
- *Unknown, Dive Coaster | History, 2020, https://en.wikipedia.org/wiki/Dive_Coaster*
- *Matt N, Alton Towers visitor figures through the years, 2020, https://towersstreet.com/talk/threads/alton-towers-visitor-figures-through-the-years.4640/*
- *RollerCoasterDataBase (RCDB), Oblivion | Alton Towers | Staffordshire | United Kingdom, 2020, https://rcdb.com/777.htm*
- *Towers Expert, Alton Towers TV Advertisements (1980-2018) [16:04], 2018, https://www.youtube.com/watch?v=CJdTn764nCs*
- *Expedition Theme Park, The History of Hex Legend Of The Towers | Expedition Alton Towers [4:04], 2018, https://www.youtube.com/watch?v=eHT06qQ99TI*
- *Churnet Valley Guide, The Chained Oak, 2016,*
- *https://churnet-valley.guide/landscape/the-chained-oak*
- *Nick Sim, Tales from the Towers, 2013, p.187*
- *Michael J. Fisher, Alton Towers: A Gothic Wonderland, 1999, p.23*
- *Michael J. Fisher, Alton Towers: A Gothic Wonderland, 1999, p.29*
- *George P. Landow, Augustus Welby Northmore Pugin (1812-1852), 2008, http://www.victorianweb.org/art/architecture/pugin/eastlake.html*
- *Alton Towers Student Information Pack 2017, p.2*
- *Nick Sim, Tales from The Towers, 2013, p.24*
- *Nick Sim, Tales from The Towers, 2013, p.29*
- *Towers Times, The Earls of Shrewsbury, 2020, https://www.towerstimes.co.uk/history/from-the-archives/earls-of-*

shrewsbury/#1507565083503-62d0f6ce-4e7f
- *Nick Sim, Tales from The Towers, 2013, p.47*
- *Michael J. Fisher, Alton Towers: A Gothic Wonderland, 1999, p.164*
- *RollerCoasterDataBase (RCDB), Skytrak | Granada Studios Manchester, 2020, https://rcdb.com/2380.htm*
- *RollerCoasterDataBase (RCDB), Stealth | California's Great America, 2020, https://rcdb.com/583.htm*
- *RollerCoasterDataBase (RCDB), Galactica | Alton Towers, 2020, https://rcdb.com/1458.htm*
- *RollerCoasterDataBase (RCDB), Spinball Whizzer | Alton Towers, 2020, https://rcdb.com/2472.htm*
- *Nick Sim, Tales from The Towers, 2013, p.201*
- *John Wardley, Creating my own Nemesis, 2015, p.156*
- *TowersTimes, Big Six Challenge, 2020, https://www.tower-stimes.co.uk/history/events-archive/2015-events/big-six-challenge/*
- *RollerCoasterDataBase (RCDB), Rita | Alton Towers, 2020, https://rcdb.com/2787.htm*
- *TowersTimes, Wooden Coaster, 2015, https://www.tower-stimes.co.uk/history/the-drawing-board/wooden-coaster/*
- *BBC News, Dubai firm buys Tussauds, 2005, http://news.b-bc.co.uk/1/hi/business/4375219.stm*
- *BBC News, Tussaud's firm bought in £1bn deal, 2007, http://news.bbc.co.uk/1/hi/business/6419019.stm*
- *John Wardley, Creating my own Nemesis, 2015, p.156*
- *Nick Sim, Tales from The Towers, 2013, p.208*
- *Alton Towers Resort, Explore | Theme Park | Rides and Attractions | Sharkbait Reef by Sea Life, 2020, https://www.altontowers.com/explore/theme-park/rides-attractions/sharkbait-reef-by-sea-life/*
- *RollerCoasterDataBase (RCDB), Gravity Max | Discovery World Taiwan, 2020, https://rcdb.com/1357.htm*

• Intellectual Property Office, Case details for Community Trade Mark E10993517 | Mark Text: The Smiler, 2012, https://web.archive.org/web/20121105222548/http://www.ipo.gov.uk/ohim?ohimnum=E10993517

• John Wardley, Creating my own Nemesis, 2015, p.164

• Alton Towers Resort, Twitter | The Smiler is NOW OPEN, 2013, https://twitter.com/altontowers/status/340420548750348289

• Alton Towers Resort, Alton Towers Resort to launch world-first Rollercoaster in 2013, 2012, https://web.archive.org/web/20121020003218/http://press.altontowers.com/news-alton-towers-resort-to-launch-world-first-rollercoaster-in-2013-11705

• BBC News, Alton Towers Smiler crash: Four seriously hurt, 2015, https://www.bbc.co.uk/news/uk-32980354

• BBC News, Smiler crash: Alton Towers operator Merlin fined £5m, 2016, https://www.bbc.co.uk/news/uk-england-stoke-staffordshire-37481825

• Alton Towers Resort, Twitter | "Galactica no longer features VR due to guest feedback regarding their experience on the ride.", 2019, https://twitter.com/altontowers/status/1107295909078097923

• Alton Towers Resort, YouTube | Alton Towers Secret Weapon programme – Episode 1 Starring Elliot Crawford, 2017, https://www.youtube.com/watch?v=zCAzniyTUTU

• Amusement Today, Amusement Today's Golden Ticket Awards 2018, p.10, http://amusementtoday.com/GTA/GTA2018.pdf

• Theme Parks UK, Review: The Alton Towers Dungeon, 2019, https://www.themeparks-uk.com/alton-towers-guide/reviews/the-alton-towers-dungeon

• Unknown, Probe into Alton Towers accident, 1984, https://i131.photobucket.com/albums/p281/flipatron/docu0009.jpg

- *Nick Sim, Tales from The Towers, 2013, p.89*
- *Malcolm McIntosh, Discovering Alton Towers, 1988, p.21*
- *Towers Street, History | The park of the past | Talbot Street | Alton Mouse, 2020 https://towersstreet.com/theme-park/ride/alton-mouse/#the-altonmouse*
- *Self-guided Alton towers Garden Tour, 2020, https://www.altontowers.com/media/cs0j35gy/self-guided-alton-towers-garden-tour.pdf*
- *Adventure Shawn, The building of Nemesis at Alton Towers with John Wardley, 1993 [Uploaded 11th April 2008], [0:17], https://www.youtube.com/watch?v=hbIpgG0q2go&t=31s&ab_channel=AdventureShawn*

ACKNOWLEDGE-MENTS

I would first like to thank all of the people who were involved in reading the countless drafts of this book and have suggested invaluable improvements to the book. These wonderful people are listed below:

Joshua Warburton, Benjamin Grzeskiak, Kelly Conway, Rowena Smith, Kledion Shahini, Helen Makin and Caroline O'Callaghan

I would also like to thank all the wonderful people who have gone to the effort of archiving and cataloguing aspects of the history of Alton Towers. Without the dedication of these people to make sure that the heritage of not only the park but the Towers ruins is remembered, there would be very little appreciation of the story behind Alton Towers.

PHOTOGRAPHY CREDITS

All images within the book are the property of the writer, <u>excluding the ones listed below</u>. The following are all permitted for commercial use under the Creative Commons (CC 2.0) licence:

Gardens image:
"Alton Towers 203" by Jeremy Thompson is licensed under CC BY 2.0

<a href="https://www.flickr.com/photos/rollercoasterphilosophy/4756094861/in/photolist-8fheix-egLPTa-egSAsA-cwLqH3-egLPTk-cwLqzS-cwLqtu-egSAtQ-egLPUn-cwLqwY-n7ikJM-iFmL6R-egLPWp-egSAq7-fmEwΓT-9IIpudX-9IIzXkP-2iyA37b-niv1Pq-as2294-7Jo9Dk-9CkWLC-9DxwZp-2hom9RX-nzKEmj-cwLqNw-cwLqD7-egSAsy-cwLqRE-cwLqUs-cwLqKY-d7xsZ9" target="_blank">"Alton Towers 203"</a> by <a href="https://www.flickr.com/photos/rollercoasterphilosophy/" target="_blank">Jeremy Thompson</a> is licensed under <a href="http://creativecommons.org/licenses/by/2.0" target="_blank">CC BY 2.0</a>

Corkscrew image:
"the Corkscrew, Alton Towers, July 1993" by alljengi is licensed under CC BY-SA 2.0

<a href="https://www.flickr.com/photos/27718315@N02/9537284585/in/photolist-fwM5r8-oD1G4j-3GGdu-4PbrYo-4P8WYv-4Pecj7-4PdvuS-4PagiD-4Paakc-oD1K9h-4P82Uz-4PeX5U-4Pgewd-4P7Uba-4PeCHh-4PcSvs-4P7hhc-4PfbrC-4Pfrt1-4PbxuG-4Pg6Z3-4Pbz6v-4PfDCq-4P7XPn-4P8yZk-4PdNcq-4PachK-4P9Ppp-4P9bHa-4P9ExD-4PbrSL-4PbWYk-4Pgbgw-4P8qgp-4P7qkP-4PfiKQ-4PawAi-4P8knF-4Pc5on-4PbmXP-4PbuqH-4Pey7J-4Pc8sH-4PbDP4-4Pc6QV-4PfNcy-4PaJ8X-4Paza2-4PbRuJ-4PbPvQ" target="_blank">"the Corkscrew, Alton Towers, July 1993"</a> by <a href="https://www.flickr.com/people/27718315@N02/" target="_blank">alljengi</a> is licensed under <a href="http://creativecommons.org/licenses/by-sa/2.0" target="_blank">CC BY-SA 2.0</a>

Alton Towers ruins image:

"alton towers" by Roger Blake is licenced under CC BY 2.0

<a href="https://www.flickr.com/photos/rogerbarker/2502393029/in/photolist-4P8qgp-4P9Ppp-4P7qkP-4PfiKQ-4PawAi-4P8knF-4Pc5on-4PbmXP-4PbuqH-4Pey7J-4P9bHa-4Pc8sH-4PbDP4-4Pc6QV-4PfNcy-4PaJ8X-4Paza2-4P9ExD-4PbRuJ-4PbPvQ-4PfJaL-4PaX6a-4Pa5yT-4P8s5n-4Pfk9J-4PeVfh-4P9YFF-4Pg12m-4PfGJj-4PfwUY-4PbcRH-4Pe2A7-4P8Sdx-4PbfN8-4PaCEv-4Pg2yG-4PfA6w-4P9AQH-4P99UM-4PaZGB-4P9RVv-4PfF9s-4P89n8-4PbFs6-4Pfu19-4P8KJr-4P8aGR-4P7k6x-4Pby34-4PfyPA" target="_blank">"alton towers"</a> by <a href="https://www.flickr.com/photos/rogerbarker/" target="_blank">roger blake</a> is licensed under <a href="http://creativecommons.org/licenses/by/2.0" target="_blank">CC BY 2.0</a>

ABOUT THE AUTHOR

Jack O'Callaghan is a theme park enthusiast from Manchester, England. At the time of writing, he has visited 18 different theme parks and ridden 285 different Rollercoasters. To this day, Alton Towers is still his favourite theme park in the world.

Jack's favourite rides include *SheiKra* at Busch Gardens Florida, *Nemesis* at Alton Towers Resort, *Icon* at Blackpool Pleasure Beach, *Journey to Atlantis* at SeaWorld Orlando and *X* at Thorpe Park Resort.

Jack's hobbies include Theme Parks, Chess, Maths and Architecture.

The author has had the honour of meeting two Rollercoaster designers in his life, John Wardley and John Burton- of Alton Towers Resort and Thorpe Park Resort, respectively.

The book's author, Jack, at the Alton Towers Hotel.

Printed in Great Britain
by Amazon